This book given to:

_____

From

_____

Date

_____

ACKNOWLEDGMENTS

With my heart full of love, I wish to thank the following:

My husband and soul mate, Rick, for his continued support and faith in me. I could not have experienced so many wonderful author moments without you!

To the beautifully talented artist, Kimberly Young, for bringing one of my dearest stories to life, thank you. It has been a joy and positive learning experience working with you!

To my oldest grandchildren, who inspired this story over fourteen years ago! You each own a piece of my heart and will always be my grandbabies no matter how old you grow. Each of you has been a special gift to me. Please know you are deeply loved today and always! May your lives be full of love and adventures as you enter the adult world.

Never Stop Dreaming!

Nana's Precious Kittens

Written by
Diana DelRusso

Illustrated by
Kimberly Young

Rain drops tapped lightly against the window pane as Precious snuggled deep into her pillow. Nana had placed it perfectly on the window seat of their old vintage home.

Precious loved this spot. This is where she would lazily watch the squirrels run up and down the one hundred year old pine trees in the front yard.

Nana and Precious had lived alone in the old farm house for many years. Nana raised her from a tiny kitten and watched her grow into a beautiful, golden-red mama cat.

A few years ago, Precious had her first litter of kittens. There had been two of them,
a boy and a girl.

The boy looked a lot like Precious, with his brown paws and a golden-red coat. The girl was mostly white with patches of orange. Nana had found a loving home for both Jacob and Sophia.

Now, Precious was expecting kittens again, but this time Nana had to go away on a trip. She did not want to leave Precious behind, but could not take her along.

Nana did not want Precious to be alone. Their nice neighbor agreed to look after Precious while Nana was away.

"Come Precious" Nana whispered, "It is time for me to go and I want you to eat your dinner before I leave on my trip. It's getting cold outside so you need to stay indoors and keep warm while I am gone."

Precious sniffed her food, then slowly crawled back onto her pillow. Through the rain drops, she watched the taxi drive down the street with her loving Nana inside.

Later that day, the neighbor came by to check on Precious.

Without warning, Precious darted past her feet. Out the front door she flew!

"Precious come back here!" the neighbor cried out. "You should not be out in this rain. It is too cold for you out there."

Precious kept on running down the street.

The neighbor was so concerned, she called Nana right away and told her what had happened.

Nana called her friend, Kade the veterinarian, and asked him to look around for her Precious cat. He promised to do the best he could, but after several days there was still no sign of Precious.

Winter came early that year. The rain continued to pour, and the temperature grew colder every day.

Precious ran down one street and up the next looking for her loving companion, but Nana and the taxi were nowhere in sight.

Precious was soaking wet and tired. She found a large bush that was low to the ground and crawled far underneath it to get out of the rain.

She slept for a little while until the pain in her tummy woke her. Could it be time for her new kittens to be born?

Precious tried to crawl out from under the bush to go home, but the pain in her tummy was too strong and she lay only partly under the shelter of the bush.

As each kitten was born, Precious grew weaker. She tried her best to clean them and nurse them. Finally, the last kitten latched onto her and Precious could get some sleep.

Precious woke later to find that she had five new kittens to love. They were a little golden-red like her with some brown on most of them.

One female was brown and white, one blonde, one dark brown, and one red. The smallest kitten was the only boy, and he was red with the same dark brown front paws as his mother.

Precious kept her kittens protected under that bush for many days while the rain and wind grew stronger. She had not eaten and was growing weaker. Snuggling her body around the five tiny kittens, she tried her best to keep them warm.

When the sun finally came out, Precious quietly crawled out from under the bush. She slowly sniffed around, searching for something to eat.

She noticed a small child drop his ice cream cone on the ground. Precious waited patiently as the child's mother took his hand and led him back into the store. Desperately, Precious licked the ice cream from the ground, then returned to her sleeping kittens.

With each passing day, Precious knew she needed to take her kittens home. She was sad, because she also knew that she had too many kittens to carry.

Fearful of leaving even one behind, she decided to care for them under the safety of the bush. Precious continued to find very little to eat outside that store. As her kittens grew larger she grew weaker.

One morning, when the kittens woke, they found their mama asleep. They could not wake her up, and she could not feed them.
Frightened of the rain, the five little kittens snuggled against her and went back to sleep.

As the days went on, the kittens grew hungrier and they began to peek out from under the bush. The rain had stopped, but the wind was very cold.

The kittens' hungry tummies led them away from the safety of the bush and out into the world. They stayed close together as they strayed farther and farther away from their mama.

Soon, the kittens found shelter from the wind in an old wooden box near a fence. They were hungry, tired and cold.

The four female kittens huddled together with the tiny male kitten and hid from the weather. There, they slept and waited. They did not know their mama could not come and help them.

When the sun began to shine, the kittens wandered out of the box and into the alley. They saw a large, red tom cat that looked a little like their mother. They began to follow him and copy the way he was drinking some spilled milk.

The kittens were so hungry, they started to drink up all the spilled milk, and the tom cat got angry. The hair on his back raised up and he stretched out his front paws and hissed loudly. The kittens were startled and ran back to the fence, where they huddled together in their wooden box.

While the kittens were sleeping, they heard a loud bang. They watched as the big tom cat knocked over a trash can and started to dig around for food.

When the tom cat was gone, the kittens rushed to the trash can and began eating the morsels of bread, meat and cheese that were left laying around. After they had their fill, the kittens returned to their box for a nap.

As days went by, the five little kittens continued to follow the beautiful tom cat up and down the alley. They ate very well on the baker's bread crumbs, and the butcher's meat and cheese scraps, but most delicious of all was the fresh, spilled milk from the dairy.

The kittens were growing fast and strong. They were learning how to jump, climb and hide as the store owners chased them away.

When Nana finally returned home from her long trip, she found her friend, Kade, waiting for her on the front porch with the town's librarian, Haily. Haily began to tell her how she accidentally dropped her car keys near a bush at the corner store's parking lot. When she looked under the bush, she found more than her keys.

Tears rolled down Nana's cheeks as Kade explained how he and Haily took Precious to his office. He told her how Precious was too weak from having her kittens, and being out in the rain and cold for so long. Unfortunately, he was not able to save her. He was also not able to locate the kittens.

Nana immediately enlisted the help of her neighbor and all of her friends to begin searching their small, vintage town for any signs of her precious little kittens.

They searched the abandoned saw mill near the creek. They walked along the creek searching around trees and under bushes. They searched the neighborhood park and playground. There were no signs of Nana's precious kittens.

While Nana and her friends were resting at an outdoor café, the butcher's wife, Erica, came rushing toward them shouting, "I saw them. I saw your kittens!"

She told Nana that five small kittens were traveling up and down the alley with a large tom cat, getting into the trash cans and making a mess. When she reached for one of them, they all ran through a hole in the fence and got away.

The kittens were fast asleep, early one morning, when they heard a loud, chilling cry.

They rushed to the back door of the dairy, where they found the tom cat caught in a broken wicker milk crate. Four kittens worked quickly to free him, while one kitten licked his face to calm him.

For the first time, the tom cat did not run away from the kittens. Instead, he led them all to safety as the dairy owner came after them, swinging his broom.

Everyone in town started calling Nana with sightings of her mischievous kittens, but each time Nana went to get them, they were gone. Nana knew she had to find a way to gather her kittens and bring them home, soon, before they got hurt.

Nana and her friend decided to set a trap to catch her wild little kittens. The dairy owner set a bowl of fresh creamy milk inside of Nana's special basket. Soon, the kittens came for their daily drink of milk. While the kittens lapped up their milk, Nana gently closed the lid of her basket and secured it.

The five kittens were startled and began crying loudly. As Nana and her friend were carrying the basket home, they noticed a large tom cat following in the distance. Nana kept looking back at him. The way he moved reminded her of Precious.

Nana had previously prepared a safe and cozy place for the kittens out on her screened porch. She laid soft pillows and blankets on the floor. She put a tall cat tree in the middle of the room with lots of hiding places in it. She wanted her kittens to feel safe and happy there.

When they arrived home, she opened the basket and watched as the kittens sheepishly crawled out. She watched two of them go straight to the bowl of milk she had placed there. She laughed while two more played hide and seek in the cat tree. She wondered why the littlest one did not come out of the basket at all.

She spoke softly to the littlest kitten as she reached her hand slowly into the basket. To her surprise, the kitten rubbed his face against her hand and allowed her to pick him up. He licked a tear from her cheek.

A sudden scratching sound caught Nana's attention. She lowered the kitten to the milk bowl, and while he drank, she looked outside.

There, she saw the tom cat scratching at her screen door. She spoke softly to him, and thought for a moment that she knew him. Again, he reminded her of Precious. His two brown front paws, red hair and bright blue eyes all made her think of Precious' first male kitten. "Could this be the same kitten, all grown up?" she wondered.

While the five little kittens fell asleep playing in their cat tree, Nana stayed outside with the tom cat. She gave him food, milk and a soft pillow to rest on. Once he had fallen fast asleep, Nana quietly went into the house and made a phone call.

Nana phoned the family that she had given Precious' first two kittens to a few years ago. The woman told her that the female kitten, Sophie, was still with them and doing well. The male kitten, Jake, ran away several months ago, and they never found him.

When she described his coloring and markings, Nana knew this tom cat was Precious' first kitten from her last litter. She invited the woman to come see the kittens and the tom cat. Nana felt sad for the Tom Cat. She went outside to try and visit with him, but when she returned to his pillow he was gone. Nana called out for him and looked around the house and up the street, but she did not see him.

Sometimes, when Nana was playing in the back yard with the kittens, she would see the tom cat hiding in the bushes. The sun light twinkled in his big blue eyes. Nana always talked softly to him and offered him food and milk. Each visit he came a little closer, and stayed a little longer. Nana hoped that one day he would feel safe around people again, and be ready to go back to his home.

On one very special afternoon, when the tom cat was visiting, Nana gave the five little kittens their very own names. The littlest one was the only boy, and Nana called him William.

The four girls were each very different. Two were very fast. The brown one was called Chloe, and the blonde one was called Annie. Two were a little quieter. The brown and white one was called Olivia, and the reddish one was called Kylee.

Nana watched the tom cat drink his milk and whispered to him, "You were the first Precious kitten, and you took care of your young brother and sisters. You are strong and wise, and your family gave you a strong name, Jacob."

Over time, the five little kittens grew almost as big as Jacob, the tom cat. The six cats continue to play in Nana's back yard everyday, with occasional treats from the store owners. They nibble on bread from the baker, and meat and cheese brought by Erica, who also brings fresh, creamy milk from the dairy.

As for Nana, she often thinks of her Precious mama cat, and although she wishes she were still with her, she loves playing in the backyard with all of her Precious kittens.

About the Author

Diana DelRusso has been writing for over forty years, creating characters and fictional stories.

In 2007, she published her first book, *The Magical Journey*.
In 2008, she published her first Christmas book, *Pages the Book-maker Elf*. She has shared her stories with children all over the country; promoting reading and writing with her personal program, Imagination/Creation. She has created multiple fundraising events.
In 2019, she published her second Christmas book in the Pages series, *Pages Awakens the Fireflies*.
Also in 2019, she created three story coloring books and plans to create more in the future.
Now in 2021, she has published, *Nana's Precious Kittens*. DelRusso has worked with talented illustrators around the world to help bring her stories to life. With an increasing social media presence, DelRusso continues to share her books with children around the world.

Follow her website for future book release dates, appearances, events and exciting information! www.dianadelrusso.com

About the Illustrator

Kimberly Young has been a freelance artist and illustrator for many years. Using a variety of techniques, ranging from digital to traditional hand drawings, she brings charming characters to life. The scenes in *Nana's Precious Kittens* were crafted with care using color pencil and digital detailing.

Since 2002, Kimberly has enjoyed bringing multiple mediums together to create fun and interesting artwork. Her portfolio includes many corporate projects for business purposes, as well as work with screen printers and metal craft. From illustration and mural painting to logo design and packaging, she has had her hand in almost every artistic medium.

Originally from Idaho, Kimberly now travels the world with her family. They have lived and worked in 34 US States and territories, as well as 12 countries. The adventure has included planes, trains, RV's, boats, blizzards, hurricanes and volcanos, with no sign of slowing down. You can see samples of her work and reach out to her by visiting **www.artisticbynature.com**

Nana's Precious Kittens
Copyright © 2021 Diana DelRusso
Illustrations by Kimberly Young
Cover design and page layout: Praise Saflor

All rights reserved.
No part of this publication may be used, reproduced, stored in a retrieval system or transmitted in any form or by any means, electronic, mechanical, photocopying, recording, scanning or otherwise, without the prior written permission from the publisher.

Publisher's Cataloging-in-Publication data

Names: DelRusso, Diana, author. | Young, Kimberly, illustrator.
Title: Nana's precious kittens / by Diana DelRusso; illustrated by Kimberly Young.
Series: Nana's Precious Pets
Description: Redlands, CA: Diana DelRusso, 2021. | Summary: A story about a woman who raises her beloved cat Precious for many years. One day, Precious's kittens wander off to find themselves lost, hungry and cold.
Identifiers: LCCN: 2021915859 | ISBN: 978-1-7375385-2-3 (hardcover) | 978-1-7375385-1-6 (paperback) | 978-1-7375385-0-9 (ebook)
Subjects: LCSH Cats--Juvenile fiction. | Baby animals--Juvenile fiction. | Human-animal relationships--Juvenile fiction. | BISAC JUVENILE FICTION / Animals / Cats | JUVENILE FICTION / Animals / Pets
Classification: LCC PZ7.1.D4565 Na 2021 | DDC [E]--dc23

Made in the USA
Las Vegas, NV
21 August 2021